WHO AM I?

STUDY GUIDE

For foreign and subsidiary rights, contact the author.

Cover design by: Sara Young
Cover Photo by: John Michael Judah

ISBN: 978-1-957369-30-3   1 2 3 4 5 6 7 8 9 10

Printed in the United States of America

MICHAEL S CARLTON

WHO AM I?

HOW I WAS RAISED WAS NOT WHO I WAS CREATED TO BE

STUDY GUIDE

ARROWS & STONES

CONTENTS

MICHAEL S CARLTON

WHO AM I?

HOW I WAS RAISED WAS NOT WHO I WAS CREATED TO BE

BEGINNINGS ARE IMPORTANT.

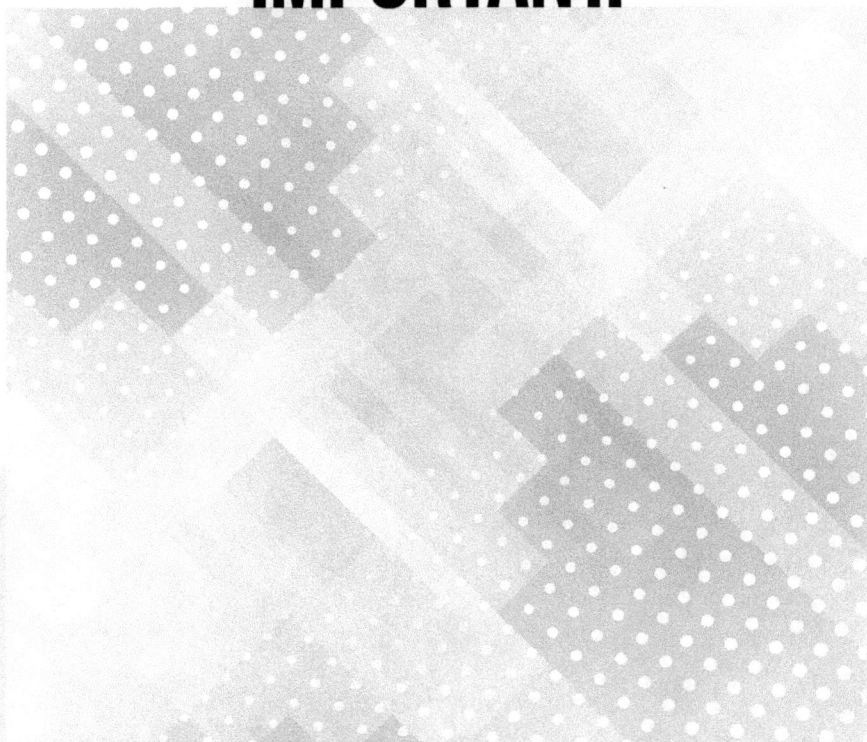

"The goal is not to be a victim, blame others, get vengeance, or keep you living in the past. The goal is to identify pain points, connect how they are playing out in your present life, and determine how you can healthily move beyond them."

READING TIME

As you read Chapter 1: "Beginnings Are Important." in *Who Am I?*, reflect on the questions and scriptures.

REFLECT AND TAKE ACTION:

Have you adopted any negative values in your youth? Where do you think these values came from?

_____

_____

_____

_____

_____

What negative values, mindsets, or behaviors have you had to discover and work to uproot in your life? How did you become aware of them?

_____

_____

_____

_____

_____

_____

Do you think the negative ways of thinking and living you mentioned above can be a part of your testimony? If so, how?

_____

_____

_____

_____

_____

> *"Confess your sins to each other and pray for each other so that you may be healed."*
>
> **James 5:16 (NLT)**

Consider the scripture above and answer the following questions:

Why do you think it's important we confess our sins to one another?

_____

_____

_____

_____

_____

_____

_____

_____

_____

What needs to take place before we can confess our sins?

_____

_____

_____

_____

_____

_____

_____

_____

_____

Do you think you're still living with some negative mindsets, or have you discovered and uprooted them all? Explain.

_____

_____

_____

_____

_____

How can you continue to make progress in eliminating negative practices and ways of thinking? Can you do it alone?

_____

_____

_____

_____

_____

Why do you think how you finish in life is more important than how you begin?

_____

_____

_____

_____

_____

Do you think God would be pleased with the progress you have made since you've found Him? Does He expect you to be perfect?

_____

_____

_____

_____

_____

NOT ME; I AM GOOD!

"The problem arises when we do not learn to cope in a healthy way or when we are oblivious to the emotional walls we put up to keep us, in our minds, safe."

READING
TIME

As you read
Chapter 2:
"Not Me; I Am
Good!" in *Who
Am I?*, reflect on
the questions
and scriptures.

REFLECT AND TAKE ACTION:

Think back to a time in your childhood when you were hurt by your parents or someone you trusted. Why were you hurt in this situation?

_____

_____

_____

_____

Was this an isolated incident or a seemingly regular occurrence?

_____

_____

_____

_____

Have you ever pursued therapy with a licensed professional? Why or why not?

_____

_____

_____

_____

If these childhood traumas go unaddressed, could they negatively affect your marriage, relationships, and family life?

_____

_____

_____

_____

> *"And we know that God causes everything to work together for the good of those who love God and are called according to his purpose for them."*
>
> **Romans 8:28 (NLT)**

Consider the scripture above and answer the following questions:

What can God use for the good of those that love Him? Is He limited in any aspect in what He can leverage for our good?

_____

_____

_____

_____

_____

_____

_____

What situations or circumstances first popped into your head when you read this verse? How do you think God may use this for good?

_____

_____

_____

_____

_____

_____

_____

_____

Why do you think so many people are hesitant to self-reflect? Is it pride? Fear? Unwillingness?

_____

_____

_____

_____

_____

Do you think discussing childhood problems with a trained therapist is more powerful than self-reflection? Why or why not?

_____

_____

_____

_____

_____

Do you think it's possible for people to put up emotional walls without realizing it? What do you think is the main contributor to this phenomenon?

_____

_____

_____

_____

_____

WHY DO YOU NOT WANT ME?

*"Despite the pains from our childhood, we must grasp
how God sees us. We are His children. Not only are
we His children, but He chose to be a Father to us!"*

READING
TIME

As you read
Chapter 3:
"Why Do You
Not Want Me?"
in *Who Am I?*,
reflect on the
questions and
scriptures.

REFLECT AND TAKE ACTION:

Is there a painful circumstance from your childhood that you only recognized the significance of in your adulthood? If so, write about it briefly below.

_____

_____

_____

_____

_____

_____

Do you think the above-mentioned situation impacted, or continues to impact, your thinking in any way?

_____

_____

_____

_____

_____

Did you ever feel insecure as a child? Was there a situation that made you question your value, worth, or your parents' love for you?

_____

_____

_____

_____

_____

> *"And I will be your Father, and you will be my sons and daughters, says the Lord Almighty."*
>
> **2 Corinthians 6:18 (NLT)**

Consider the scripture above and answer the following questions:

What is your reaction when you read this verse?

_____

_____

_____

_____

_____

_____

_____

_____

How should we live, act, and love in response to knowing this verse?

_____

_____

_____

_____

_____

_____

_____

_____

_____

Do you think that becoming secure in your God-given identity is a process or an overnight decision?

_____

_____

_____

_____

How can you better understand your identity? Is this something we do on our own, or should we lean into our Creator and Father for better understanding?

_____

_____

_____

_____

Do you think the enemy attempts to wound us and negatively affect our self-image?

_____

_____

_____

_____

CHAPTER 4

A MAN ALREADY?

"Your Father God wants to be awe-inspiring in your life. He wants to display His glory and grandeur to you, but He will never force himself into your life."

REFLECT AND TAKE ACTION:

Is there anything you think your parents should have taught you that you had to learn by yourself?

_____

_____

_____

_____

_____

_____

Did you ever feel you had to be independent as a child? Do you still feel this way in adulthood?

_____

_____

_____

_____

_____

Do you think being overly independent can hurt those around us?

_____

_____

_____

_____

_____

> *"Let me know your ways so I may understand you more fully and continue to enjoy your favor."*
>
> Exodus 33:13 (NLT)

Consider the scripture above and answer the following questions:

Do you seek to better understand the Lord's ways, as this verse states? Why or why not?

_____

_____

_____

_____

_____

_____

_____

_____

Do you think God's favor is dependent upon our obedience and heart?

_____

_____

_____

_____

_____

_____

_____

_____

_____

Do you pray for God's presence and involvement in your life? Do you want Him by your side as you live life, or do you try to do everything independently?

_____

_____

_____

_____

_____

Do you actively seek out and submit to God's will for your life?

_____

_____

_____

_____

When you accomplish things, do you take the credit, or do you give God the glory? Would He say the same?

_____

_____

_____

_____

_____

Do you believe God wants to grant you victories in life so that He receives glory? Do you believe He wants you to better know Him and live out His will for your life?

_____

_____

_____

_____

_____

AM I GOOD ENOUGH?

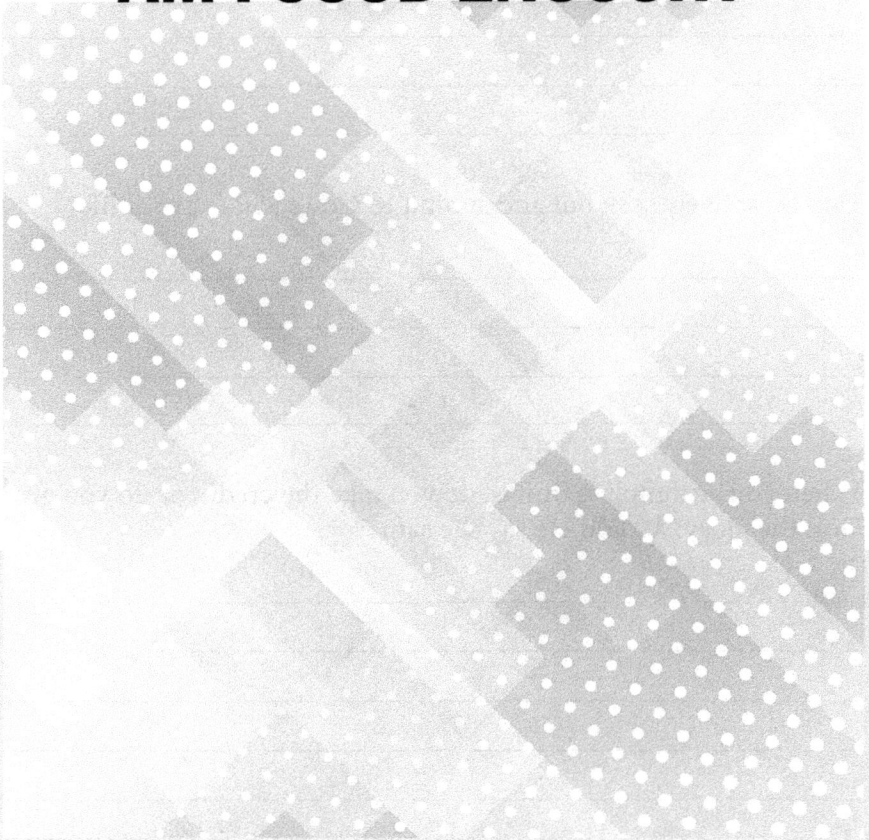

*"Insecurities and unfulfillment are
rooted in a lack of identity."*

READING TIME

As you read Chapter 5: "Am I Good Enough?" in *Who Am I?*, reflect on the questions and scriptures.

REFLECT AND TAKE ACTION:

Do you ever feel the need or desire to impress those around you?

_____
_____
_____
_____
_____
_____

In childhood or adulthood, have you ever been insulted or made to feel insecure by someone else?

_____
_____
_____
_____
_____
_____

In your own words, why do insecure people insult, criticize, and demean those around them? What causes them to lash out?

_____
_____
_____
_____
_____
_____

> *"I know how to live on almost nothing or with everything. I have learned the secret of living in every situation, whether it is with a full stomach or empty, with plenty or little. For I can do everything through Christ, who gives me strength."*
>
> **Philippians 4:12-13 (NLT)**

Consider the scripture above and answer the following questions:

Are you able to live as Paul did, with plenty or little? Do you have the same mindset?

_____

_____

_____

_____

_____

_____

_____

How should others' negative comments towards us affect us if we live as Paul said he lived in the above verse? Where does our value, identity, and security come from?

_____

_____

_____

_____

_____

_____

_____

What does success mean to you? What does it look like in your life and current situation?

_____

_____

_____

_____

_____

How are heaven's metrics for success different from the world's?

_____

_____

_____

_____

In the parable of the servants discussed at the end of the chapter, what was the master's response to those that had doubled what they were given?

_____

_____

_____

_____

Do you ever compare yourself to those around you? Do you think comparisons can negatively affect your view of yourself?

_____

_____

_____

_____

CAN I REALLY CHANGE?

*"Too many of us want freedom without releasing
our past to Jesus. We are chained to the past,
and it keeps us from moving forward in life."*

READING TIME

As you read Chapter 6: "Can I Really Change?" in *Who Am I?*, reflect on the questions and scriptures.

REFLECT AND TAKE ACTION:

Do you believe God truly forgives and forgets your sins when you ask for forgiveness?

_____

_____

_____

_____

_____

_____

Do you believe you can completely change and uproot your sinful habits with the Lord's help?

_____

_____

_____

_____

_____

Do you feel there are any areas of your life where your obedience is divided between God and the world?

_____

_____

_____

_____

_____

_____

> *"But Jesus told him, 'Anyone who puts a hand to the plow and then looks back is not fit for the Kingdom of God.'"*
>
> Luke 9:62 (NLT)

Consider the scripture above and answer the following questions:

What do you think this verse means?

_____

_____

_____

_____

_____

_____

_____

_____

Has God ever moved you to change and you delayed it out of self-ishness or sinful desire? Describe the situation.

_____

_____

_____

_____

_____

_____

_____

_____

_____

Have you ever actively asked and prayed to the Holy Spirit to show you your areas of disobedience and sinfulness?

_____

_____

_____

_____

_____

_____

_____

_____

What does it mean to be filled with the Holy Spirit? Do you think this is a one-time event or a daily request we should make?

_____

_____

_____

_____

_____

_____

_____

_____

Do you think we can change from our sinful ways independently from the Lord's assistance? Why or why not?

_____

_____

_____

_____

_____

_____

_____

_____

Do you think the enemy only attacks those who are not yet Christians, or does he deceive us and inhibit our relationship with the Lord as well? Do you think he has blinded you in your relationship with God in any way?

_____

_____

_____

_____

_____

_____

_____

_____

WHOM CAN I TRUST?

"We can navigate through the pain of being abandoned and betrayed and realize like David, that God will always receive us with open arms most lovingly!"

READING TIME

As you read
Chapter 7:
"Whom Can I
Trust?" in *Who
Am I?*, reflect on
the questions
and scriptures.

REFLECT AND TAKE ACTION:

Have you ever found it difficult to trust others after being hurt by someone? Describe your experience briefly.

_____

_____

_____

_____

_____

_____

Have you ever failed someone else who trusted you?

_____

_____

_____

_____

_____

_____

Do you feel you can unconditionally trust in God? Do you think He has ever or will ever fail those who trust in Him?

_____

_____

_____

_____

_____

_____

> *"Then I pray to you, O LORD. I say, 'You are my place of refuge. You are all I really want in life.'"*
>
> **Psalm 142:5 (NLT)**

Consider the scripture above and answer the following questions:

Have you ever felt God was the only thing you really wanted as David did when he wrote the above verse?

_____

_____

_____

_____

_____

Do you feel like God is your place of refuge? Do you feel like you can confide in Him and trust in Him wholeheartedly?

_____

_____

_____

_____

_____

What are some of the lessons we learn from David authoring the Book of Psalms whilst in turmoil?

_____

_____

_____

_____

_____

When God moves in your life, do you share His involvement and provision with others?

_____

_____

_____

_____

_____

_____

_____

How do you think God feels when He moves in our lives and we keep it to ourselves?

_____

_____

_____

_____

_____

_____

_____

CHAPTER 8

WHAT LIE DO YOU HAVE TO BELIEVE?

"If we're honest with ourselves, part of the unhealthy thoughts that replay in our lives are the lies and manipulation we have believed."

REFLECT AND TAKE ACTION:

Have you ever had trouble believing something God has told you? Do you ever find it difficult to believe the entirety of God's Word?

_____

_____

_____

_____

_____

_____

What lies from the enemy have you conquered with God's help in the past?

_____

_____

_____

_____

_____

_____

Do you think there could still be lies from the enemy that you allow to negatively affect your life?

_____

_____

_____

_____

_____

_____

> *"How joyful are those who fear the LORD—all who follow his ways! You will enjoy the fruits of your labor. How joyful and prosperous you will be!"*
>
> **Psalm 128:1-2 (NLT)**

Consider the scripture above and answer the following questions:

What does it mean to fear the Lord?

_____

_____

_____

_____

_____

_____

_____

_____

_____

What is the significance of this verse using the world "labor"?

_____

_____

_____

_____

_____

_____

_____

_____

What is the most important thing to you in your life? Explain your answer.

_____

_____

_____

_____

_____

Do you ever feel like you have to carry the difficulties of life alone? Who in your life do you feel can help you?

_____

_____

_____

_____

_____

Do you have a deeply rooted reverence for the Lord? Is it enough to seek His divine will over your own?

_____

_____

_____

_____

_____

THIS IS WHAT IT FEELS LIKE.

*". . . the journey towards health is, in fact,
a journey. You do not just magically wake
up healed and whole; it is a process."*

READING TIME

As you read Chapter 9: "This Is What It Feels Like." in *Who Am I?*, reflect on the questions and scriptures.

REFLECT AND TAKE ACTION:

Where does your joy come from?

_____

_____

_____

_____

_____

_____

_____

Where does the world think joy comes from? Is this true joy?

_____

_____

_____

_____

_____

_____

What does authority mean to you? Who has authority over your life?

_____

_____

_____

_____

_____

_____

> *"Children, always obey your parents, for this pleases the Lord. Fathers, do not aggravate your children, or they will become discouraged."*
>
> **Colossians 3:20-21 (NLT)**

Consider the scripture above and answer the following questions:

Why do you think children's obedience to their parents pleases the Lord?

_____

_____

_____

_____

_____

_____

_____

_____

What does this verse mean when it tells fathers to "not aggravate [their] children"? Do you think this applies to mothers as well?

_____

_____

_____

_____

_____

_____

_____

_____

What happens when parents misuse the authority they have been given?

_____

_____

_____

_____

_____

What are some examples of ways parents can misuse authority?

_____

_____

_____

_____

_____

How can parents protect their children from discouragement as this chapter discusses?

_____

_____

_____

_____

_____

Do you think vulnerability and authenticity are important traits for parents to demonstrate to their children? Why or why not?

_____

_____

_____

_____

_____

_____

WHO AM I?

"*My God called me by name. Every day of my life is written in His book. I am His masterpiece that was crafted in His image. I am not a mistake. I am not discarded junk. I am not unwanted. My God desires me. My God sees greatness in me. My God has filled my life with purpose. My God is my father. As you are reading this, I hope you understand this is true for you also.*"

READING TIME

As you read
Chapter 10:
"Who Am I?" in
Who Am I?,
reflect on the
questions and
scriptures.

REFLECT AND TAKE ACTION:

Have you ever questioned your identity or
who you were made to be? Briefly describe
your experience.

_____

_____

_____

_____

_____

_____

_____

What is your identity? Do you feel content
and stable in who you are?

_____

_____

_____

_____

_____

_____

How do you think people of the world estab-
lish their identity?

_____

_____

_____

_____

_____

_____

_____

> *"Listen to me, all you in distant lands! Pay attention, you who are far away! The LORD called me before birth; from within the womb he called me by name."*
>
> **Isaiah 49:1 (NLT)**

Consider the scripture above and answer the following questions:

Do you believe God had plans for you even before you were born?

_____

_____

_____

_____

_____

_____

_____

_____

How should this verse affect our day-to-day lives and decision-making?

_____

_____

_____

_____

_____

_____

_____

_____

Do you trust in the plans God has formulated uniquely for you?

_____

_____

_____

_____

_____

What needs to change in your life to fully embrace His plans instead of your own?

_____

_____

_____

_____

_____

Do you think anything can stop us from pursuing and achieving the plans God intended for our lives if we wholeheartedly follow Him?

_____

_____

_____

_____

_____

CHAPTER 11

WHERE DO WE START?

"*Our goal should be to feel a little better, respond a little better, and achieve a little more every day.*"

REFLECT AND TAKE ACTION:

Is there an area of your life that jumps out to you as a good place to start in making a change?

_____

_____

_____

_____

_____

Are there any negative mindsets about yourself you let live in your mind rent-free? Write them and make them known below.

_____

_____

_____

_____

_____

Are there any sinful habits that are prevalent in your life that need to change? What are they?

_____

_____

_____

_____

_____

> *"But the Holy Spirit produces this kind of fruit in our lives: love, joy, peace, patience, kindness, goodness, faithfulness, gentleness, and self-control. There is no law against these things!"*
>
> **Galatians 5:22-23 (NLT)**

Consider the scripture above and answer the following questions:

Which of the above fruits of the Spirit do you feel you need more of? Take time to pray and ask the Holy Spirit to help you in this area.

_____

_____

_____

_____

_____

_____

_____

_____

What is the significance of this verse stating: "There is no law against these things"?

_____

_____

_____

_____

_____

_____

_____

Do you have faith that you can conquer the sinful areas of your life with God's assistance?

_____

_____

_____

_____

_____

What kind of a man or woman do you want to be? How do you want God to see you?

_____

_____

_____

_____

_____

What needs to change to make the above possible?

_____

_____

_____

_____

_____

Write down where you wish to be five years from now. What will be the key differences between you today and you five years down the line?

_____

_____

_____

_____

_____

www.ingramcontent.com/pod-product-compliance
Lightning Source LLC
Chambersburg PA
CBHW070050100426
42734CB00040B/2977